MW00368407

THE WAY OF THE CROSS

THE WAY OF THE CROSS

The Path to New Life

JOAN CHITTISTER

Art by Janet McKenzie

ORBIS BOOKS
Maryknoll, New York 10545

Founded in 1970, Orbis Books endeavors to publish works that enlighten the mind, nourish the spirit, and challenge the conscience. The publishing arm of the Maryknoll Fathers and Brothers, Orbis seeks to explore the global dimensions of the Christian faith and mission, to invite dialogue with diverse cultures and religious traditions, and to serve the cause of reconciliation and peace. The books published reflect the views of their authors and do not represent the official position of the Maryknoll Society. To learn more about Maryknoll and Orbis Books, please visit our website at www.maryknollsociety.org.

Published by Orbis Books, Maryknoll, New York 10545-0302.
Manufactured in the United States of America.
Designed by Roberta Savage

Library of Congress Cataloging-in-Publication Data

Chittister, Joan.
The way of the cross : the path to new life / Joan Chittister ; art by Janet McKenzie.
pages cm
ISBN 978-1-62698-044-0 (cloth)
1. Stations of the Cross. 2. Stations of the Cross in art. I. McKenzie, Janet L., illustrator. II. Title.
BX2040.C45 2013
232.96—dc23

2013003212

To Pat Cuccia and Cheryl Baugh,
Faithful and loving women,
Because of whose commitment to the Word
Everything else is possible.—Joan Chittister

With profound gratitude to Helen and Clifford McKenzie,
my mother and father who loved me unconditionally.—Janet McKenzie

Contents

The Passion of Christ

Janet McKenzie

This interpretation, a quiet glimpse into the humanity of Christ, does not acknowledge the spectacle that surely accompanied Jesus to his death. The exuberant din from the gathered masses and street noise made by excited children and barking dogs surely assaulted his mind and thoughts—the sounds of life soon to be denied to him.

Here the cross is not the familiar wooden version, large enough to bear a man's weight with nails big enough to support a person—a cross able to snuff out a life. The cross in this series appears only as a dark horizontal or vertical form, one Jesus struggles to pick up and keep upright as he falls. Although a reference to the cross is an essential component of the Passion, with meaning beyond simply a place to die, my focus is on Jesus.

Mary's presence is the counterbalance to Christ's suffering. It is she, his Blessed Mother, who reaches for him, caressing his face in their final goodbye. In that moment it is as though they are alone, her love for him so exquisite that it blocks out all else. And, after Jesus is taken down from the cross she mourns, cradling her son close to her heart as she did so long ago.

Surely Jesus was in prayer, in conversation with his Father, as he approached his death. Prayer, our intimate dialogue with God, belongs singularly and privately to each one of us, and this is the essence behind this work.

Introduction

Every journey through life is a deeply personal and forever unpredictable one. No two of us ever do it in quite the same way. Except for one thing: However stable our circumstances, however solid our formation, however fortuitous both our beginnings and our immediate circumstances, we are all of us at the mercy of change and beholden to the fragility of time.

The bends and curves of personal experience move back and forth in seamless fashion between the startling luminance of life at one moment to the dark night of the soul at the next. On one day, life, it seems, is unambiguous. Everything has been settled, once and for all. The job is secure, the marriage is firm, the house is in the right place, the future is assured. Nothing is too much for us. No clouds threaten the sense of achievement or compromise the flow of blessings we have come to expect. But then suddenly, on the next day, it all begins to unravel, it disappears and nothing is certain anymore. Confusion, consternation, obstruction, uncertainty set in, obscuring our vision, disturbing our hearts. Very little of life feels right now; the sense of failure, the fear of the unknown weighs us down.

At times like that, where do we turn for understanding? Where can we look in those dark, lonely moments to find hope? When there is no way out but through, when there is no clear course beyond the murk of it all, what do we do then? Where is the model of strength we need to stay the course, to live through the pain, to assuage the hurt, to find hope in the future? Where in all the in-between-places of life are the signs of promise that beckon us beyond pain to its burgeoning fulfillment?

One of the oldest devotions in Christianity, the Stations of the Cross, attests to the ongoing human effort to understand the place of suffering in the human's search for resurrection from death to life that is part and parcel of what it means to be alive and grow and become our best selves as we go.

If nothing else, the ongoing popularity of the Stations of the Cross across the ages is a sign of the universal awareness of the presence of pain in life. However much effort and resources the human race puts into the elimination or cure of pain, both physical and emotional, pain simply does not go away. It is part of life. Its inevitability and its burdens, its necessary contribution to the growth of human wisdom and its call to human growth remain. It is not only part of the spiritual process of human development, it is essential to the process of stretching us to the very breadth of our souls.

No wonder then that the popularity of the Stations of the Cross as a perennial devotion can be traced across the ages. There are signs of the practice in Jerusalem as early as the third century when pilgrims began to trace the way of Jesus from the garden of Gethsemane to the hill of Calvary.

By the fourteenth century, the number of "stations" or stopping points along the route from Jesus' condemnation in the house of Pilate to the finding of the empty tomb had become identified and ordered. By the sixteenth century, the devotion had spread to the universal church. Now, in the twenty-first century, the stations are still a public statement of faith, compassion and conviction that even the daily deaths of life can lead us to the stuff of spiritual resurrection time after time on our way to the fullness of life.

Clearly, Jesus' last great gift to the church is to show us what it means to lose everything in life and still go on to more of it.

The Stations of the Cross, unlike many traditional private devotions—novenas, for instance—are not designed to beg God for favors or special attention of any kind. They are instead simply an excursion through the hard moments of life, the very ones that are demonstrated in the life of Jesus himself.

They are not valuable to us because they concentrate on suffering, as if life were a burden to be carried, a problem to be solved, rather than a grace to be lived to the edges, drunk to the dregs, squeezed dry of learnings and insights and wisdom. Instead, they give us a model of how to live life when our own struggles are unavoidable and life seems most oppressive, most unfair, most impossible to bear.

Then it is the Stations of the Cross that remind us again that there is new life at the end of every daily death.

Knowing that Jesus, too, has gone the way of injustice, fatigue, failure, public rejection and loss before us gives our own present struggles new hope and new light.

But suffering is not all or only or even primarily what the Stations of the Cross are really about. We are not, after all, the people of the Cross. We are the people of the Empty Tomb, Alleluia people, the people who know that every step we take leads to new life, however bleak, however distressing our situation seems at the time. It is in faithful and lifelong attention to the Stations of the Cross that we may come to see that at every abject junction of life we are being called to look again, to deal with life with fresh and untried capacities, to discover dauntless ways of dealing with pain and coming to wholeness again. The stations are about finding in the life of Jesus a deeper model of how to deal with the torment, the loss, the rejection, and the injustice that are weighing us down, crushing our spirits, challenging our faith.

We pray the Stations of the Cross in both good times and bad in order to learn how to live. Then, as the years go by, we may come more and more to realize in ourselves a life lived in hope, not despair; in courage, not in fear; in an awareness of blessings rather than locked into a tomb of bitterness.

THE STATIONS

1. Jesus Is Condemned to Death

The Experience

The look on the face of Jesus in McKenzie's rendering of the first station says it all: Accused, judged, and condemned Jesus stands totally undone, emotionally drained, more by the charges against him than by any act of physical violence. Here, in this first station, we see what actually happens to the person who is publicly incriminated by a system that is clearly arrayed against him. It is one of those rush-to-judgment moments when no one really bothers to ask or let alone to listen to your own explanation of circumstances or your understanding of it or even your distance from the issue at hand.

It is as much a shocking time as it is a sad one. This moment is about the accusal of the innocent. This is the disarming of the strong. This is the plight of the person who has no recourse with which to rebut the charges, who knows no advocates strong enough to be any kind of protection in a case based more on prejudice than fact.

This is the struggle of those whose goodness has forever been without question but who has, for whatever reason, suddenly become suspect. With one blow, the work of a lifetime of character building begins to crumble.

At that moment, the inner sense of impacting personal presence

so carefully constructed for years, from one stage of life to another, simply begins to collapse, to break down, to come apart one brick at a time. The world turns on the innocent with a vengeance—on the woman who protests unjust pay, on the foreign worker seeking survival from starvation, on the homeless ones who lack either the skill or the support it takes to move up a shaky social ladder, on the person with an impeccable distinction but no way to disprove the evil of this unprovoked attack.

There is nothing for a person to do then but to move, head in hands, through the channels of pain that come with any show of resistance and defiance of a system too often closed to those who need it most.

The hard-won reputation for goodness and honesty we worked so hard to build up around us frays in plain sight. The public image of dignity and worth, so precious to us all, goes to dust in the wake of rejection that comes with disdain. What dies in us is the sense of confidence, of public bearing, that until now, at least, has carried us through all the difficult moments of life.

It is a moment of inner pain and loss greater than anything anyone can possibly do to hurt a person. It is not the pain of the body. It is the pain of the soul. Once we have lost dignity, been robbed of our reputation, have lost everything dear to us, have been closed out of society and social acceptance, what is left of the person is only a body covering a shell of a soul.

The Call

The spiritual challenge of the moment of public rejection is to maintain a strong sense of being in the hands of God. Drawing our personal sense of self now out of the well of the past, we go on because of what we know God wants us to be rather than what we want people to think we are. Stripped of social approval, I come face to face with my need to be honest with myself. Who I know myself to be will determine what I must do to become whole again. It is inner growth we are about now, not social cosmetics.

We are being called to become the best of ourselves at the worst of times. How others treat us is not nearly as important now as what we know ourselves to be. We will not despair of God's mercy for us. We will not betray either our hope in God or our dignity of self. We are called, in the face of the injustices against us, to refuse to be less than we have always been spiritually. We are being asked to remember that the God who created us, as scripture says, "wishes us well and not woe." We are called to rely on that, to be a sign to all that with God we can withstand anything.

The first station, condemnation without cause, is a call to put our trust in God when the world around us has abandoned us, when there is little of our own internal resources left on which we may depend, when we find ourselves despised by those with whom we most wanted to succeed.

The Model

Jesus, the model of inner strength at a time of serious public pressure, stands tall and strong in the face of injustice. He acknowledges the moment but does not give in to it. He does not betray either his faith in God or his own consciousness of the will of God for him. Instead, he stands up to his accusers with dignity and strength. He does not grovel; he does not beg. He brings himself full and entire to a false trial and he questions his accusers as much as they question him. He deals with the injustice arrayed against him with dignity, with honesty, with stolid commitment and with undying determination to continue to say the truth—all the way to the end.

The Rising

For everything that dies in us at a moment like this, there are other things that come to new life in us, as well.

The first station of the cross requires us to examine our entire philosophy of life. Jesus is condemned to die because he defied the standards of both the state and the religious establishment in which he lived. To both he brought a truth they did not want to hear. He set out to witness to the love and justice of the God of all creation: Jews and non-Jews, women as well as men, underlings as well as the professional types of his time.

Surely we are called to do the same, to speak our truth with clarity, simplicity and conviction. What must rise in us in times like these is a clear commitment to what must be, to the truth that must surely come if the will of God is really to be done on earth and to our role in bringing it.

He cured on the Sabbath, mixed with foreigners, taught theology to women, played with children, questioned every law, chose people over ritual every time, and never made institutional authority a god.

He threatened the establishment with his incessant attempts to build a better world and they set out to destroy him for it.

The question with which the first station confronts us is a stark one: What is it in life for which we are willing to be condemned? The goal in life is not to avoid condemnation. No one does. Life's great challenge is simply to decide who will condemn us and why. If we were better people, perhaps, we would be condemned more often.

Most of all, when we are condemned for the right reasons, the first station reminds us, we know we will not be there alone. Jesus will be standing beside us, full of pain for our sake, but head up and unyielding.

2. Jesus Takes Up His Cross

The Experience

Who does not understand this second station of the cross? Who is it that cannot feel the depth of the emotional anguish that goes with it? In fact, who has not lived through it themselves in some way, somehow in life? After all, the unpredictable burdens of life are part and parcel of being alive. Difficulties are everywhere and at every level of existence: The relationship ends, the friends go, the success goes to someone else, the illness comes on quickly and fells us without warning.

Clearly, there are some things we simply cannot avoid. These things disappoint us, of course. They bear down on our lives in very real ways. They change us, sometimes for life. They try us to the very marrow of our souls and they are not to be dismissed lightly. No doubt about it: It takes courage to carry them well. It is one thing when the tribulations of life come from our own hands. But when we ourselves did nothing deliberate to bring them on, the sting is even worse.

The truth is that there are two distinct kinds of crosses. The first comes to us out of nowhere, without warning, not at our own hand, just one of the circumstances of life. The second kind of cross

we make for ourselves. Inadvertently, perhaps, but consciously nevertheless.

What ought not be part of life, however, is the cross that comes from the hand of another determined to oppress and designed to kill spirit or body or both.

Having preached the world of the Beatitudes in a world of violence, having healed the hopeless, questioned the system, opened his arms to the outcasts and challenged the world to live differently so that life would be different for everyone everywhere, the cost of it all in jealousy, resentment, anger and ill will comes quickly. It is this burden of malice that is the cross Jesus reaches out to take hold of here. This is the cross he did not want but was willing to accept so that the world might see another way to be alive.

The Call

This station asks us all a very direct question: For what would you be willing to risk your life? What crosses do you yourself take on, knowing the risk, understanding the cost and being committed to the consequences? The call of the second station is no small mission. It requires us to live life consciously, to know what's going on around us, to take some kind of responsibility, however small, for the welfare of others, for justice in the part of the universe we call our homes, our country, our world.

This station calls for involvement in life. It calls us to leave the isolation of spiritual narcissism that treats the spiritual life as some sort of personal comfort zone designed to protect us from the world we live in. It requires us to make the journey from Galilee to Jerusalem ourselves, healing the sick, raising the dead and bringing the Gospel to a world long dead of soul.

The Model

What we see in Jesus in the second station is a striking challenge: The second station of the cross teaches us that commitment costs. To choose one path in life from another is to choose its consequences.

Real commitment implies that, like Jesus, we carry the burdens of our choices in bad times as well as good, on difficult days as well as easy ones, in the face of opposition as well as at times of great public or popular support.

We pay the price of being true to ourselves, of doing what must be done when doing what could be done would be so much easier. When Jesus took up the cross, all hope for a miraculous end to an impossible situation was over, both for him and for us. The tariff of truth told in behalf of justice is often pain.

The question with which the second station confronts us is a dangerous one: Having begun a good thing, will I pay the price to bring it to fulfillment? It's so easy to talk of great virtue, so simple to begin a thing. It's seeing it through the questions and criticisms and doubts and despair that really counts.

In this second station, we see a critically conscious Jesus embrace a cross unbearably beautiful for its meaning, unbearably bleak for its pain.

The Rising

The very act of accepting a cross for the sake of another gives rise in us to the best of ourselves. In that act, the heart of Jesus awakens in us and we become new of soul again. It is the moment in which we rise from the grave of a world that long ago gave up the ideal in favor of the pragmatic, the just in favor of the profitable.

The very impulse to choose the best over the comfortable or the secure is sign that the resurrection has begun in us. Every action of Jesus to stretch the vision of Israel—the choice of the menstruating woman over the dictates of the law, the choice of the children over the prestigious adults, the choice of the Roman soldier over the officials of his own system—made him more and more an enemy of the system. But it also made him more and more clearly a sign of the presence of God on earth, so will it do the same in us.

3. Jesus Falls the First Time

The Experience

Somehow or other, a kind of "bread and circuses" approach to life has begun to permeate modern society. Everything we do is about winning something or measuring one person against another or garnering goods in great quantity, not because we need them but in order that others can't have them. We make life one great competition, a win-lose situation, a measuring stick by which we parade our value to others and, saddest of all, use those same things to convince ourselves of our own value. As if what we get outside of ourselves is any measure whatsoever, any indicator at all of what is at the soul of us internally.

We dedicate our lives to collecting things that have little or no permanence, even for us. We position our own value on having bigger houses, more money, a job with a private office, a collection of adult toys we soon tire of and, of course, a party list of prestigious strangers, guests who are more our "contacts" than our friends. All of those things function simply to prove our social status, at least to ourselves. And we call it life. Until one day the fire happens, or the mortgage comes due, or the stock market crumbles under our feet. Or worse yet, one of our own—a child, a spouse, a sister, a relative—lets the brand down and disgraces us in public or embarrasses us in the church circle or becomes a public figure even more impressive than ourselves.

Then reality strikes. The matchstick tower we have made for ourselves and upon which we sit for all to see begins to sway a bit. Then what is left? Then what do we do? Then where can we go to get a new perspective that can distinguish real life from what is nothing more than a bogus attempt at it?

The Stations of the Cross could be a very good place to start. There at the third station all pretense ends. Reality sets in.

We ourselves have set out to glorify the crucifixion of Jesus. From a distance of over two thousand years it is easy enough to forget the crowd shouting "Crucify him" during the greatest of the Jewish holidays. We have lost sight of the fact that it was during one of the most crowded feasts of the year where all of Israel heard of his downfall, his disgrace, his loss of status even among the peasants. They, after all, are the kind of people who would later say, "I know not the man" and "Others he saved; himself he cannot save." It is easy to look at the third station and forget that Jesus the wonder worker, at the height of his popularity, fell in the mud on a dirty garbage-strewn street of a sandy village in the Middle East. It is easy to forget now that he looked anything but regal, that the crown was made from the branches of a thorn bush, and that this is the one who said, "Come, follow me." It is easy to ignore the necessary question now: Will you? And if you do not follow this one, whom will you follow?

The Call

The day we fail in the face of everyone we have ever wanted to hear applaud us is the day of truth. That is the day we finally begin to determine what is really important in life. It is a time for deciding what separates winners from losers in life. Then, it is time to pick one route or another for ourselves.

But such a time is not an easy time. It means that we must be prepared to re-examine everything. We must ask ourselves what impels what we do—ourselves or the others who cheer as we go by. Now we are

forced to look again at our goals in life. Are we living to make the world a better place or ourselves a more powerful one?

When we miss the cheers—when we care more for the cheers of some than for the jeers of others—we have come to the point in life where we need to check our attitudes as well as our actions. We need to ask ourselves how we really feel about the poor, the women, the immigrants, the one who is not like us. We have to determine what systems we really identify with in our hearts—the rich or the poor, the local or the international, the denominational or the universal. And we must ask those questions of ourselves with searing sincerity.

An experience of failure requires us to turn life upside down, to turn ourselves upside down. The process is an important one. As a result of it, we may well discover that what others may call success may actually be failure. It means that we must accept the fact that what others call failure may indeed be what rings through the ages as true. It is the dialect of the cross in which courage means more than security and the coming of the reign of God means more than public success.

The Model

The sight of it is devastating: he is on the ground now, one knee in the dirt, clinging to the cross itself to hold him up. What can we make of him now—the healer, the prophet, the Chosen One? Where's the power? Where now are the crowds who shouted, "Hail, King of the Jews"? The pain of the moment is about more than the pain we see on Jesus' face. We have some misgivings, some painful moments at this station ourselves, because we know the answer to those questions. The answer is that the image we hold so dear, the image of prophet, of rabbi, or healer and miracle worker, the image of the hero—is gone.

The third station of the cross reminds us that success often looks like failure. We do things that seem to falter, to fizzle, to miscarry, only to realize later that the floundering was part of the process. If Jesus had not fallen under the cross, who of us could possibly have come to see that what appears to be collapse may actually be the beginning of another insight into success?

"What we call failure is not the falling down," the proverb says, "but the staying down." The fact is that Jesus could have stayed down where he fell, having decided that he'd gone far enough, leaving it to his executioners to drag him the rest of the way. But he didn't. Instead, he showed us all that the important things in life are worth struggling for to the end.

The question with which the third station confronts us is a simple one: Is the struggle of my life worth enough to struggle for to the end? If I am not engaged in a large enough life issue, no amount of struggle can dignify the paltriness of it. On the other hand, if the struggle of my life is equal to the Gospel, to the coming of the reign of God here and now, no amount of duress can ever deter it.

The Rising

The gift of life that comes with the third station is a simple one. What grows in us as we sit with this station is the awareness that reality is greater than either image or fantasy. It is coming to know that life consumed by the cosmetics of public appearance is, whatever it is built on, short-lived as well as endemically false. Money can only take us to the edge of the grave, power only lasts as long as people allow us to have it, sooner or later things go to rust and physical attributes will all eventually turn gray, get brittle, go dim and soft and thin and fragile.

To accept reality as it is, to give ourselves for the lives of others, is the only thing that can enlarge our stature and will not diminish us as we go.

4. Jesus Meets His Mother

The Experience

This fourth station is a life lesson far beyond either the dull or dour particulars of life. This station is about the place of love in life.

It is one thing to have zest enough for the future; it is valiant to recognize reality and to embrace it with spirit. But it is something else entirely to find ourselves alone in the midst of the painful but defining moments of life—birth, death, castigation, humiliation, failure and rejection. With love we can do anything, even the clouded parts of life, so tenebrous but at the same time so necessary, so commonplace. But without love, we can only die long before death takes us.

Even in the Stations of the Cross we find this comment on human need and human gifting. Even here, in the life of the one we call "the Jesus of history, the Christ of faith," there is a clear sign of the need for support, of the place where care becomes a universal part of the human enterprise.

There is no bravado in the stations, no affected disregard for pain, no display of sophisticated disinterest from bystanders. On the contrary. People stand like honor guards in the street to weep as the procession of cross and criminal goes by. And there in the midst of them, Mary the mother of Jesus sees her good son persecuted in order to satisfy a few autocrats fearful of his impact on others. Surrounded by people struggling with the loss of hope that the loss of Jesus represents, Mary reaches out through her own unbearable pain to give support here.

No, the stations are not a gladiatorial script imposed on the ignominious execution of this first-century rabbi. Jesus is suffering, struggling, falling in the street. The onlookers, unlike the crowd outside the house of Pilate during the trial, are not screaming for blood. These are people strong enough, involved enough, to give sign to the world of the wrong being done in their midst but at the same time powerless to do anything about it.

Central to it all is Mary, the mother, the one who never goes away regardless who says what about this savior of the people who is at one and the same time the enemy of the state, the apostate of the law. Mary who herself braved the negative reactions of both religion and culture to have this child refuses to deny him now. Love for the outcast is the gift she brings to the moment. The proclamation of presence is the sermon she preaches. Disgraced in the eyes of the population who have abandoned him, she does nothing to hide her love or her continuing commitment. They have leaned on one another all their lives. No way to change that now. They will simply both suffer this cataclysmic moment together, she for him, he for her, both of them for the sake of the world which they serve.

The Call

The fourth station is the station of unconditional love, the kind of love that cannot be diminished under any conditions, regardless of any accusations, whatever the cost to the self. This is the love that is godly—that does not judge, that stands by, that knows the best and believes in it. It is the best a human can do, whoever the person, whatever the crime.

To grow in the spirit of the fourth station, we must learn to do the same, to love without boundaries, to love without censure, without condemnation. Love lets the rest of the world do that. It is for the lover to simply accept what is and stand by to see it through.

The Model

The face of Jesus cradled in the hand of Mary is an icon of the unity that bonds souls in times of shared pain. There is a oneness here that is above and beyond the biology of birth. There is in the common bond between them a unity of hearts formed by the pangs of pain. Having borne his body, she is now bearing the weight of his soul in hers. There is no recrimination here, only acceptance. There is no distance here, only a melding of hearts that is beyond anything merely physical. Now, he knows, they are bearing together the beginning of a whole new world.

The fourth station of the cross teaches us the freedom that comes with real love. Jesus and Mary meet under the worst of circumstances. He has become an enemy of the state, an outcast from the synagogue. She is a widow left alone in a male world without the sustenance of her only son and no visible means of support. Both of them, in a way, are condemned to death. But she does not beg him to change his life for her sake, she does not spend herself in self-pity and he does not tailor his life given for others to give only to her.

At first, the reality of that jars the soul a bit. Shouldn't he live his life to please her? Shouldn't she demand from him his conversion to the ways of the world around him, for his sake, of course, but for hers, as well? Isn't that what good sons, good parents, good friends, good lovers do? The answer is yes only if we believe that our children belong more to us than to God and only if we believe that anyone—our teachers, our parents, the people we love in life—has more claim on our souls than God does. The answer is yes only if we think that

love requires molding a person to ourselves rather than changing ourselves, giving ourselves, so the good of the other is realized. In this case mother and son love one another enough to respect the place of God in both their lives.

The Rising

The question with which the fourth station of the cross confronts us is Why do we love and how well? If we love another for our own sake, that love is doomed for both of us because it stands to twist both of us into shapes that are not our own. The truth is that there is no one who can ever satisfy all our needs. The moment of new life happens for us when we can love the other and at the same time let them go. Let them free to become the wholeness of themselves. Allow them to do what they are meant to do in life. And let them do it better because they feel the support of genuine love every step of the way. Love like that can never fail us because the freedom we give to the other to become frees our own becoming as well.

5. Simon Helps Jesus Carry His Cross

The Experience

The fifth station confronts a rigidly stratified world with the great crossover moments of life. What are we supposed to do when we find ourselves face to face with something no one wants to get involved in but what we also know must be done? It's more common a problem than we like to think.

You and I, for instance, come to realize that two children in our block are living with their homeless mother in a car. What do we do: Forget about it and hope some agency will come along and deal with the problem? Call the police? Find a tiny efficiency apartment and pay the rent for a year? Join an organization that concentrates on finding shelter for homeless people? Obviously it isn't that there's nothing that can be done about a dilemma like this or, as a matter of fact, about most of the social quandaries that are beginning to crowd our headlines, swamp our cities, pollute our country. There are myriad ways to get involved with anything we want to get involved with. It's not that there are no solutions. No, the problem really lies in being willing to get involved in the first place.

So, why don't we? Because. Just because, that's why. Because we're too busy, too tired, too old, too something whatever to care, perhaps.

Too removed from the problem to make it our own. Too convinced that anyone who has worked as hard as we have in life could surely take care of themselves without our help. Too ashamed to risk our present social image by retelling family stories of what it cost to come up in the world one small step at a time now that we're there.

Clearly, someone else's second-class social status can easily dim our own. So we hurry by.

Simon of Cyrene was hurrying by, too, they tell us, when Roman soldiers, fearful that their prisoner would die before they had a chance to crucify him on Calvary, forced him into helping Jesus lift the heavy cross.

There is no word recorded in scripture about how Simon responded or why he hadn't stopped to help in the first place, but we can guess: He was embarrassed, perhaps; irritated, perhaps; repulsed, perhaps. And all those things are exactly the proof that we are being called to do something. The fact is that when we feel like that about something, it is sure proof that we are being called to respond to it—because, obviously, we need as much help in dealing with this thing as does the person we're avoiding on the street.

The Call

The call of the fifth station is a clear one: The function of the follower of Christ is to get involved. The people we call outcasts in a society riven by poverty, war, racism, and sexism are the crucifixion figures of our time, bowed down under the weight of injustice, suffering from a system that has made them outcasts, invisible, pariah.

The people we do not see, have not known, or never associate with on the back streets of our cities need our voices raised in their behalf, our hearts softened in their behalf, our souls opened to lives far unlike our own.

The Model

The fifth station of the cross demonstrates for us the power of presence in the lives of the poor and oppressed. Being where suffering is, associating ourselves with it, standing with those whom society has condemned is a great and gracious witness. At life's greatest moments we choose it. At other times, it is thrust upon us when the state wants more tax money to support the needy, a relative's child has nowhere to go for a while except with us, a neighbor turns to us for help we did not freely offer and do not want to give. We're overworked, we're run ragged as it is, we don't want to get in the middle of something we can't get out of easily, we don't want to change the already strained pattern of our own lives. But sometimes, if we're lucky, we find ourselves in one of life's great acts whether we want to be there or not. Then we so often discover that it is not so much what Simon did for Jesus as what Jesus did for Simon that counts. Then we learn to recognize that by the very fact of our coming face to face with the other, Jesus is changing our life, too.

The questions with which the fifth station of the cross confronts us are, What are we being called to do for someone in need right now for which we are a disinclined observer? What does the situation have to offer us as well? When we open our hearts to the other in need, we are very likely to discover that our own hidden needs have been healed in the process.

The Rising

The determining dimension of new life in us at this station is the rise of new consciousness in us. We become more alive because we learn to let more life in than we are accustomed to. We have, in fact, come to live very protected lives. We have blown a great bubble around our-

selves—often more pious than really holy—which, until now, we never recognized was there.

We go through life meeting, partying, working with the same people. We dig a moat of church-going, civic engagements and neighborhood gates around us to the point that we never see what is on the other side of those barriers. We keep the drawbridges of our small worlds raised and run the risk of missing the Jesus-figures who walk by looking for our help, our presence, our companionship through life.

6. Veronica Wipes the Face of Jesus

The Experience

The story of Veronica, whose act of compassion left the wounded face of Jesus imprinted on the veil with which she wiped his bleeding face, is a mixture of tradition, legend and devotions that developed over the centuries from one end of Europe to another.

There is no ascertainable historical accuracy attached to any of the tellings, let alone to any of the "veils" themselves, but there is a great deal of spiritual truth to be recognized here. The truth is that nothing we do for the suffering other ever goes unnoticed or unnoted. The kindness we bring to great moments of pain and grief marks us and lasts forever not only in the heart of the person whose pain we assuage but in our own soul as well.

The woman Veronica, unlike Simon, is said to have stepped out of the crowd voluntarily as Jesus stumbled by under the weight of the cross in order to wipe the sweat and grime from his eyes. That the image of the face of Jesus remained on the veil she used to do it endures from one century to the next without a single shred of data to support the story. And yet, clearly, it is not the historicity of the story that counts after all these centuries.

Veronica has become part of the universal spiritual psyche in the

Stations of the Cross because the witness of Veronica to the power of witness stands for all to see. What does Veronica do? Not much. What does Veronica mean to the spirit of the stations? Close to everything.

Here is a woman who will not allow the story of the journey to Calvary to be romanticized, to go untold, to be overlooked or forgotten. The image on the veil remains forever a reminder of the unmitigated horror of which injustice is capable.

The woman's veil stands as mute witness to the depths of the demonic present in the human condition once we permit it to be unleashed. The veil remains a witness to the crime of all times—the destruction of goodness at the center of us, in us, around us forever.

Compassion and witness take the stage of our hearts here. Her act of compassion, we know, puts us to shame. How often do we stop to mend the broken in the streets? Her unblinking witness puts us on notice: for the sake of what life lesson would we draw attention to ourselves? For the sake of the ongoing valor of the world, to what kind of care would we bend our own lives so that the world would not forget? Stolid in her performance, the woman stares into the heart of humanity, challenging us to justify such an act as this senseless, unjustified act of brutal violence. Neither can be erased. Not the brutality, not the courageous compassion. Both of them prod our conscience and break our hearts forever.

The Call

In Veronica's mild, womanly way there is embedded a striking call to authenticity, to being what we are meant to be, to doing what must obviously be done no matter who approves, no matter who thinks this is neither the place nor the time. It takes the breath away to imagine stepping out in the middle of a street gang to wash the face of a beaten boy. It takes an inner strength beyond the average level of integrity to speak up for women in a crowd of conservative churchmen. It takes a kind of spiritual insanity to question the corporate practices everyone else takes for granted at the cocktail party.

But it is precisely that kind of commitment Veronica takes for granted. She haunts us with it. She pursues us with it. She insists on it. Nowhere are we to allow the Jesus figures of our day, the poor and the oppressed, to suffer where we are. It is a mandate more demanding than sinlessness.

The Model

The sixth station of the cross calls us to realize that compassion is the counterpart of justice. To fail to practice mercy in the presence of injustice is to neglect half the face of God. Jesus does not resist the journey to the cross but he does respond most to the act of comfort in the midst of oppression.

It is not enough, we learn here, to harbor a sense of righteous anger when the poor are oppressed. It is necessary to reach down and lift them from the pit of their despair. It's a false zeal that focuses on the addiction but ignores the addict, that calls others to family values but gives no child beyond our own a helping hand, that deplores discrimination but avoids gays and lesbians. The plight of Jesus here is a clear model for us: Justice punishes criminals, yes, but mercy refuses to ignore their needs. Justice seeks the vision but mercy makes it real. Justice follows the ideal but mercy recognizes the weakness in ourselves and so holds the weaknesses of others in a tender hand.

The Rising

Veronica walked out of the crowd of curious onlookers and horrified spectators and bloodthirsty zealots and performed a work of mercy, no questions asked, no judgments rendered. And for her trouble, she left, tradition tells us, with an image of the face of Jesus on the very towel she used to give him relief.

The meaning is obvious. Every time we make life physically better for someone else, the face of Jesus becomes clearer and clearer in us. We become more of what we are meant to be. We rise up out of a petty past and become a clearer, cleaner, brighter picture of the face of Jesus ourselves.

The question with which the sixth station confronts us is, Who is there, whose life you deplore, that you have reached out to help?

The image that Veronica takes away on her veil is an image of serenity, of soulful repose in the midst of human chaos. The veil does not scream at us. It does not sob. It does nothing to draw attention to itself. Instead, in its steadiness it draws attention only to us, to those who see it, to challenge us. You, the veil says, you. Will you yourself ever do anything for those who live in the centrifuge of violence and deprivation, to raise them up, to give them hope, to stop the pain they breathe?

7. Jesus Falls the Second Time

The Experience

The problem with life is that it never really gets resolved. What's more, the same issue that tested our mettle the first time we attempted it leaves us in doubt that we should ever attempt it again. The things that confuse us the first time we deal with them are just as likely to make us wonder about them the second time around as well. Certainty is a chimera. All we really know for sure is that what we did last time in dealing with a problem either did or didn't work. Will the same thing work again? Who knows?

This station touches the deepest part of that truth. Faced with something that bested us the last time we met it, the whole thought of dealing with it again can make the heart go weak. How can we even dare to think of getting up and going on again? In fact, why even bother to try?

Doubt is one of the great spiral challenges of life. We live with it at one level or another every day of our lives. We suffer from it even more when what we did to conquer it the first time was more accident than strategy. What if that same kind of blind happenstance does not save us now?

It is doubt that brings us to wrestle with the very foundations upon which our life is built. Can we do this thing? Should we do this thing? Why is this thing even worth trying to do? Why even try to do the impossible—to stretch ourselves beyond the normal, the average, the clearly possible?

And if we try it again and we fail, then what?

The second effort makes or breaks the average person. The second effort either deadens the soul to the rest of life or redefines us to ourselves. The second effort becomes the "I can't" trap, the point after which we never try again, or it becomes the "I can" truth that lifts us to a new level of courage forever.

Here in the seventh station we see Jesus fall again, more tired this time, more dejected this time, even less committed, perhaps. Why not just die in the dirt? Why try to get up at all?

It is the eternal question of life in general. More important, it is the question of the spiritual life, too.

The Call

The spiritual life is not a walk in the breeze. It is the solemn sacred effort to make life count, to make good on what we set out to make of ourselves, to become the wholeness of our spiritual selves. And the energy it takes is exhausting. But the spirit it takes to keep going on past the physical, psychological, spiritual ability to go on is of the essence of greatness.

The call to holiness, to witness, to commitment is undeniable now: The Jesus who falls a second time gets up a second time determined to see this cross through to the end.

The call to live our lives to the pinnacle of the truth within us, however impossible it may seem along the way, is a clarion one. We are each here to give our best and give our all in the service of the will of God for us. There is no going back. There is no staying down when we fall down. We bother to get up and try again because we said we

would. There is only the answer of Isaiah: "Here I am, Lord. Send me" (Isaiah 6:8).

The Model

The seventh station of the cross reminds us that obstacles are a regular, a normal, even a necessary part of life. It is the obstacles we meet along the way, the problems we overcome, the setbacks we survive that measure the value of the enterprise at hand. They give us both perspective and wisdom. Once we have stumbled but continued the race, collapsed but not quit, fought and endured, no pain is too much, no cost too heavy to pay for what is worth our laying down our lives for it.

The questions with which the seventh station confronts us are grave ones. Is there anything important enough in our lives, our goals, our faith for which we are willing to endure both pain and doubt, even when going on seems to be impossible? Is there any pain worth more than the desire to run away from it? And if not, what kind of spiritual life can possibly be sculpted out of a life lived only on the surface of glitz and the passing pleasures of the moment?

The Rising

We are risen to a new level of life when we come to understand that the ultimate purpose of life is to focus ourselves on something worth struggling beyond our strength to attain. It is the moment of freedom in us. Then it doesn't matter whether we win or lose in the process. What is important is that we give ourselves to something big enough to grow beyond ourselves to gain.

The very act of throwing ourselves into the wrestling match of the soul makes us a beacon of hope for those who come behind us. There is no such thing as weakness for those who are strong enough to keep on trying.

As Mary Pickford said of those moments, "Today is a new day. You will get out of it just what you put into it. . . . If you have made mistakes, even serious mistakes, there is always another chance for you. And supposing you have tried and failed again and again, you may have a fresh start any moment you choose. . . ." The message is a clear one: It is the choices we make that determine who we really are in the end. It is not the mistakes we make that make us small, it is choosing to surmount them that makes us great.

Being willing to get up again in the attempt to live life well is the resurrection moment promised in the seventh station.

8. Jesus Meets the Weeping Women of Jerusalem

The Experience

This station we understand in this day and age only too well. In a digital world people fall in and out of favor too quickly for us to remember their names—if we have even had enough time to learn them in the first place. Social media and entertainment sites update with glee the list of public figures—politicians, entertainers, artists, scions—who have fallen from public grace. They tell us from one day to another who's out and who's in, who's up and who's down. If we never understood the truth of what past generations have taught us about the vulnerability of a person's public image, we know it now as never before. The messages they gave us were ominous: Reputation, they told us, is a very fragile resource to depend on in a world that makes and breaks them with impunity. Guard yours carefully. Just one false step, they insisted, and the public estimation it takes a lifetime to build can be permanently damaged.

Then the shunning begins, sometimes in very subtle ways. People who want to be photographed with you on one day refuse to be seen with you the next. Invitations to all the parties stop. Street conversations get shorter and shorter.

Or worse, the shunning gets to be total isolation. No one even nods to you in the streets anymore. The bantering in the office ends. The email disappears. The foursome for golf or cards or tennis or fishing never seems to get together anymore. And no one—no one—crosses the invisible social line to reach out, to listen, to stand by. The pain of it slays the soul. It's a dark time in an even darker day.

Avoidance becomes the order of life. The public's fear of guilt by association stops life in mid-flight. Friends disappear; acquaintances deny knowing you at all. The shunned inhabit a world of one when friends have never been needed more.

All of which is why this eighth station of the cross is such a stunning one.

One moment Jesus is hailed and applauded, lauded and followed. Then, arrested without cause, the crowds begin to shout for his blood. He is pushed and pulled, jostled and ogled on the street. Surrounded by soldiers, crushed by the weight of the cross, bleeding and exhausted, he has gone from revered teacher and wonder-worker to ignominious criminal, outcast, derelict in the society.

And then the miracle happens. The world's most unlikely group of supporters steps into the scene. They were not the apostles and disciples who had enhanced their own reputations by their association with him. They were not a group of people whom he had healed in the course of his ministry. They were not people of influence or the upper class whose testimony and character witness he might have needed. No, they were no one of importance at all. They were, in fact, just women. They were a rag-tag body of women whose brave presence made it clear that Jesus who had been condemned by the upper class was, nevertheless, a hero to the underclass. In fact, it was for that very reason that the upper class had to get rid of him.

The women weep for Jesus, condemned and censured for all to see. But the call is for more than compassion.

The Call

The call of the eighth station is two-fold. First, we are challenged to put down the judgments and the prejudices that turn societies into social prisons. We are called to open our lives to the souls of those whose social behaviors repulse us but whose state is more the result of the social system itself than it is of any act of their own. Then we are called to change the society in which this kind of oppression and injustice is permitted to go on unchecked and even unnoticed.

This station calls us to look again at those we ignore. But this time we are called to look with care. We are called to really see the situations in which they live. We are called to forego the criticism that condemns people whose lives and circumstances we do not know to the margins of society forever. We are called to realize that we ignore these people to our peril as well as theirs.

The Model

The eighth station of the cross compels us to consider the long-range implications of our actions. It is the counterpoint of the sixth. The sixth station reminds us that mercy must prevail. The eighth station tells us that justice must come or we will all suffer for the lack of it. To seek justice without doing mercy, to do mercy but not to seek justice is, in both instances, to live a partial life. To feed the hungry but fail to question the policies that make people hungry or leave people hungry neglects the real issue.

Some of us find it easy to judge and condemn. Others find it easy to serve and support. The truth is that support without judgment is compliance with evil. "Don't weep for me," Jesus tells the women of Jerusalem. "Weep for yourselves and your children." The implication is clear: If this society continues on the road that it is on now, it dooms

itself to the effects of such policies. Don't weep for the people on death row, in other words, weep for the kind of society that would stoop so low as to become what it hates.

The question with which the eighth station of the cross confronts us is, Do we really reject what we call sinful or do we really reject only the sinners themselves? The question brings us to face ourselves at our deepest, darkest core. This station calls us to go beyond what is to what must be.

The Rising

To begin to see beyond the person to the environment, to the social policies of a system, to the circumstances for an understanding of life is to begin to live life to the fullest. Then, we are less likely to allow individuals to bear the sins that belong to us all. Then, we rise to a new level of wisdom. We do more than live ourselves; we begin to give life to others, as well.

9. Jesus Falls the Third Time

The Experience

There is something about the taste of failure that damps the spirit. But when the failure comes time after time, as it does in this ninth station when, having already fallen twice, Jesus falls again, then the very marrow of a person's soul is frozen in place. What is the use? we say. Why bother? we begin to wonder.

At these moments, there are parts of life that die in us. Our dreams wither a bit. What we had hoped to be able to do has come undone. What we had planned for years to do is no longer in the realm of the possible, we think. Everything we were sure we could do alone, could do at all, could do maybe as well as anyone else if not better, has come to dust.

Then, there is nothing left for us to do but to accept the failure and retire from the fray or to reject the failure and risk the thought of being forever second class, not quite up to it, behind everyone else in the race of life.

There is a third option, of course, and that is to go on anyway, go on despite the effort of it all. There is a classic short movie making the rounds of the digital world. In it, a handicapped child runs a marathon with his class of normal runners. They all outrun him. But he is the one

who wins. Why? How? Simply by crossing the finish line—not with them but long after them. After all of them had done what was easy, he did what looked to be impossible for him, what had indeed seemed almost deadly for him—he simply ran the race all the way and crossed the finish line. And, in crossing it, he showed the world that it is not what we do "pretty" that calculates the depths of a person's soul. It's what we do beyond all the odds that matters.

Life is a matter of going on beyond the possible. When the work is draining but we do it despite that because others will suffer if we do not, we are fully alive. When the great ideal of our hearts is far, far beyond our resources, but we strive for it regardless, we are fully alive and the world is better because we were here. When we continue to do what is difficult for us because it is worth doing, then we have become the fullness of ourselves. Then there is nothing we want to do that is impossible; like the child in the race, it will only take us a little longer to do it.

The Call

The call of the ninth station is to refuse to give up doing what the world needs to have done simply because we do not succeed at it on the first try. The call is to see failure as part of the process of our lives and to learn from it accordingly.

There is no call as important as refusing to quit doing what is worth doing.

The Model

The ninth station of the cross demands that we persevere in doing good, in being what we must be, in holding our course even when the pressures around us mount to break our spirits. Just when we think we have come to a plateau in life, things change. The job disappears, the home begins to fragment, sickness slows us down, relationships break our heart. It all seems useless. All the efforts seem to be for nothing. Then it is time to realize that there is nothing we now take for granted in life that wasn't first considered either untenable to do or insane even to think about. That's when getting up and starting over becomes one of the miracles of life. When Jesus falls, Jesus certainly wants to quit. But Jesus' life was about accepting the consequences of love and justice, whatever that might be. Quitting was not an option.

The questions with which the ninth station confronts us are challenging ones: Are we about something impossible enough to be worth every effort of our lives? And if not, why not? What great contest, what inconceivable race, is life about for us?

Since when did complacency become a virtue when love is in need of repair and truth is in need of proclamation? If we are not involved in something that demands the unstinting best of us and threatens the very core of us, what is life about?

The Rising

When we refuse to give up, when we go on trying—whatever the odds against success—something new is born in us. Instead of a sense of failure, the very matter of trying recreates our sense of purpose, our sense of commitment, the perpetuity of the dream. What does it matter if justice never comes, as long as we refuse to abandon the ideal? What happens to the vision of equality if we never let go of our demand for it? And on the other hand, what will happen to the will of God for the world if we will doggedly go on giving our own lives to it so that others may know its fullness in their own?

To rise to new life in our own time, it is necessary that we rise to every call of every station to which Jesus leads us.

10. Jesus Is Stripped of His Garments

The Experience

There is something about the thought of being stripped naked in public that is particularly chilling. Clothing, after all, makes us what we are: the professional, the academic, the official, the hard-working, the accomplished, the stylish, the straight-forward, the credible. Without clothing, the very notion of personage disappears. Once stripped, there is no dignity left. There is no status, no solemnity, no real person left to see.

It is a devastating thought: George Washington, naked. Therese of Avila, naked. Thomas Merton, naked. Dorothy Day naked. Nelson Mandela naked. Hillary Clinton, naked. Franklin Delano Roosevelt, naked. We wince and turn away. It is simply too much to imagine: the great, the powerful, the admirable, the spiritual, the mighty—all naked. If anything reduces a person to nothingness, it is nakedness. No doubt about it: The stripping of Jesus is a terrible thought.

Once naked, the image of the rabbi is gone; the wonder-worker is destroyed; the Son of God has become a memory.

But there are other kinds of strippings as well. We can be stripped of our offices, or stripped of our secrets, or stripped of our masks. We can, in other words, be reduced to social dust after years of social dignity.

The pain of that is almost unimaginable. It is a pain far worse than physical suffering. It is the pain of the total loss of self.

Onlookers deride and demean. Friends distance themselves. Family members feel the shame as surely as if they themselves had gone through the stripping.

Who doesn't know the feeling of public exposure, of the loss of respect, of the end of a public face?

The meaning of the tenth station of the cross is clear: It is psychological obliteration, the deep down fear of every thinking human being from the point of grade school humiliations to disgrace at the pinnacles of life. Far worse than time in prison is the publicity that precedes it.

And for what use?

The Call

The spiritual summons of the tenth station is to the development of genuine humility. The call is not an enticing one to most Westerners whose social goals consist primarily of superiority, primacy, advantage and transcendency. To even think of wanting less, society leads us to believe, is a kind of betrayal of the self. "Be all that you can be" is more an expectation than encouragement.

As a result, somewhere along the way, humility, one of the ancient virtues, has come to be seen as the suppression of the self. Humility has become confused with humiliation.

But never doubt that humility and humiliation are not synonyms. Humiliation defaces the soul. It leaves us stripped and vulnerable in a world of mockery. But humility, true humility, makes humiliation impossible. Humility is self-knowledge. It is the state of mind achieved by total openness before the God of unconditional love. The humble person is the one who knows who he or she really is and puts on no airs in an attempt to pretend otherwise. Humble people know, too, that God knows exactly who they are and loves them totally nevertheless.

The humble person cannot be humiliated because the humble person does not wear a mask to begin with. What you see in them is what they are, and what they are is what you see. They have no fear of exposure because they have never pretended to be anything more, anything other, than the most stripped down presentation of themselves implies. They put on no airs, they do no artful pretending, they tell no social-climbing lies; they refuse to make their costume themselves. They are more than policeman, more than bishop, more than financially secure, more than superwoman. They are simply one more person among the persons of the world. We know them when we see them and we love them at first sight.

The Model

The tenth station of the cross confronts us with the inevitable in every life. Somewhere along the way, we each get stripped of what we have spent our lives acquiring, of things closest to our hearts, of possessions or positions that made us who we thought we were. Then, thrown back upon ourselves, we are left to discover who we have really become. It is a frightening moment, often an embarrassing one, always a difficult one. So much of life is spent attending to the show and glitter, the masks and trappings, the externals of our personal identities that we fail to notice what is lacking inside of us. The problem is, of course, that we don't miss what we don't have within us until we need it most. Then the lack of dignity, of self-containment, of simple joy, of deep sincerity, of spiritual serenity, of holy trust, of genuine humility become glaringly apparent. It's only at the point when we realize who we are not that we are ready to become someone worthwhile.

The question with which the tenth station faces us is, What is underneath the garments of pomp, authority, dignity and wealth that we have so carefully cultivated around us? Anything at all?

The Jesus who stands before us naked and unashamed, dignified

and full of conviction is calling us to pay more attention to who we are than what we have so cunningly conspired to pretend to be.

The Rising

When we have finally stopped the posturings and personal exaggerations of life, the freedom that comes with being honest with the self and open with others leaves us perfectly free. Now, nothing can possibly shame us again. No one can say anything about us that we have not already admitted, if not to others, certainly to the self. Now we cannot be slighted because we know who we are. We cannot be embarrassed by the past because we have already embraced and confronted it. We cannot be left to the vultures of life because there is no way left to pick us to the bone that we have not already reckoned with ourselves. It is a moment of great liberation. It is a moment of new life.

Being willing to be the self and nothing more is the beginning of truth, the essence of humility, the coming of peace.

11. Jesus Is Nailed to the Cross

The Experience

The words "Jesus is nailed to the cross" trip lightly off the tongue. Not to worry. After all, it's Jesus on this cross, and God will take care of him, we think. Or to put it another way, the whole event has taken on the character of play acting: It's Jesus—who is God—and so the pain of it really doesn't hurt him. It's not the real thing. The humanity of Jesus is forgotten and the cross becomes more symbol than real.

The problem is that, as a result of that kind of spiritual trivialization at the eleventh station, we stand to lose the very meaning of the moment. As if our crosses are "real" but Jesus' crosses are not and so there is nothing we can learn there.

The problem is that we fail to understand the cross until we really have one.

Every difficult thing in life is not a cross. A lot of things are difficult in life but that does not make them crosses. Some jobs are difficult by nature: Being a forest ranger in a tower alone day after day can certainly be tedious. But if I love being out in nature, if I'm grateful to have a job in the midst of so much beauty, if I love people but enjoy the silence of the woods, however long my hours or isolated my position, the job is not

a cross. To say otherwise is a serious misnomer. A cross is that which we do not choose and do not want. It is outside the normal order of life. It is what confounds our plans or disturbs our dreams. It is anything that wrenches life away from our plans or hopes in a truncated or destructive or pitiable way. It is where we would not go but cannot avoid.

Or to put it another way, the cross is what we choose by choosing something else. To choose to have a child is to choose to suffer their suffering as well as your own. To choose to stand for justice is to risk suffering from the brutality of those who have the power to oppress. To choose to work for equality is to feel the blows of those who protect the structures who deny it. To choose to tell the truth about those who have the authority to have me barred from every similar position in the system can certainly be the cross that comes with the compulsion to be ethical, to be honest, to be committed.

Jesus' cross was not some kind of petty inconvenience. It was a distortion of a great life and even greater plans and in great proportions. It was the cutting off of life in the very thick of it. It was the cost to be paid for confronting the authorities of both synagogue and state in an attempt to make both institutions what they were meant to be for all our sakes.

Nor are the real crosses of our lives minor irritations or teasing tests of our faith in God. The cross is not an exercise in temporary discomfort. It is life-changing.

Crosses are permanent. They are about things that very likely can never be altered. Being nailed to the cross simply forestalls all other possibilities. To nail someone to a cross means that there is little chance for change, this situation is forever. The cross of taking care of a seriously brain-damaged child is that, however much the love or sense of responsibility, this situation will never change. As long as the child lives—2, 4, 8, 20, 40 years—total care will be necessary and a parent's entire life will be given over to it.

Clearly, being nailed to a cross is far different from a temporary misunderstanding or a fluctuating organizational aggravation.

The cross brings with it a sense of finality, the judgment of forever. There is no going back from here. Jesus is nailed to a cross from which there is no return. The glory days are over. The followers are scattered. The entire enterprise seems lost. It is the bleak and final moments of the dream. There is no way whatsoever to plumb the depths of such depression in the human soul.

The Call

The call of the eleventh station is the call to faith, to believe that a loving God is also present in darkness so deep that nothing can possibly assuage it. It is the call to faith in the God of Timelessness in a time of total defeat. It is trust that the God who created us and loves us will hold us up through this moment so that the darkness does not break our hearts.

The Model

The eleventh station of the cross brings us all to face the moments when we know we must do what we do not want to do and, more than that, feel we cannot possibly do, however it changes our lives.

When what we know to be right exacts more from us than we think we can give, then Jesus nailed to a cross is our only hope that one day the cross we seek to avoid will have been worth the climbing. The cross is what we feel when the project flounders and fails without reprieve, when the love disintegrates, when the position is over, when all the supporters go away, and when life in the future appears to be shapeless and gray, totally deprived of the heartbeat of hope. Then we begin to realize that life's real problem does not lie in being nailed to a cross, it lies in choosing a cross that is too small to even attempt to justify being nailed to in the first place. When we spend our energies on small things, when we spend our lives chasing dreams that do not satisfy, we suffer as much to lose them, but for far too small a reason.

The question with which the eleventh station confronts us is whether or not we are spending our lives, our hopes, our emotions on something great enough to make the pain of losing them worthwhile. The great task of the spiritual life is to choose to spend it on something big enough to risk the pain of its loss.

The Rising

There is a great freedom that comes when the cross we refuse to accept becomes the cross we embrace. When we give up the struggle against life, life begins to lighten in us. We become indestructible. Nothing more can hurt us now. Being handicapped is not a death knell anymore. We learn to live in ways we never imagined possible and find ourselves made new. Being alone is not a burden now; it is an opportunity to start over again. Being blocked by one impasse in life, we discover whole new ways of being alive. We find new life in the small deaths of the day. We sink into the ultimate liberation. Now there is nothing in life but the freedom of choosing again.

12. Jesus Dies on the Cross

The Experience

What is worse than the actual event of death is the awareness of the degree of loss that comes with it. Simply announcing that someone has had "a peaceful death" does nothing to damp the pain of it. When the death is a violent one, the deprivation—the sense of having been able to do nothing to have stopped the pain—burrows down into the center of the soul dark and endless.

Violent death, natural or not, haunts us at night and plagues us during the day. It stops time at the moment before the loss. It suspends us in an orbit of pain. Now what?

What can possibly fix the lives that are left to mourn the dead who die out of time and at the hands of the uncaring, the indifferent, the institutionalized lackeys of the system?

Entire lives of multiple people can become disoriented by the loss of a loved one. Death is about far more than simply the life of the deceased. It marks in every life the moment after which nothing else is ever quite the same. In some cases, a whole system, an otherwise strong network of friends, can disintegrate without so much as a moment's notice after the death of the leader, the glue, the cement of the group.

The question now becomes How is it possible to go on alone? How is it possible to compensate for, let alone replace, what has been lost? What is now denied the lives of those whose own life depended on the deceased in ways far beyond the economic, far beyond the mere matter of getting through the day, is not only irreplaceable, it is paralyzing. It is enough to stop the natural flow of life completely.

And then, too, what about the person whose life has been cut off, like black twine in dark night? What about the dead dream that can never now be completed? What happens to those who dreamed it together or trusted in its coming, whatever it was?

These are empty times for everyone. These are times that crush spirits and stop hearts, abort plans and blur visions deeply. Life hollows out, one way or another, for everyone concerned.

These are times that stretch faith in life to the break point. These moments suspend time for everyone.

The Call

The call to us at a time when great pieces of the future crumble in life is not so much to faith as it is to hope. Depression is the seedbed of hopelessness, the loss of surety that life must still somehow be full of good, however impossible it is to remember it, to see it, to trust it at this moment.

Hope does not tell us that soon life will be the same again as it was before the loss. No, hope tells us that life will go on, differently, yes, but go on nevertheless. Hope tells us that the pieces are there for us to put together, if only we will give ourselves to the doing of it.

When Jesus dies on the cross, something entirely different rises. And that something is the call to us to make the best in life live again.

The Model

The twelfth station of the cross brings us face to face with the finality of defeat. Sometimes things don't have a happy ending in life. They just grind on until loss becomes the new normal.

Sometimes we fail. There are things we are not suited to do, however much we want to do them. Then, valor lies in simply being willing to begin again, somewhere else.

Sometimes we're beaten. Others are more talented, perhaps, or better prepared, or hungrier in their pursuit of the present grail than we are any longer able to be.

Sometimes we're lost. Sometimes we're humiliated. Sometimes we're misunderstood.

Sometimes we are abandoned by the very people we love most in life and who we thought also loved us. At that point, without doubt, something in us dies.

Then we learn that there's no going back to things that once were but are no more. The old breath goes out of us and all we can do is to surrender to the dark. It is not a pretty moment. It can take all the energy we have.

The question with which the twelfth station confronts us is an awesome one: Am I able to accept the daily deaths of life, both the great ones and the small, knowing that death is not the end of life, only its passing over to something new in me? Hopefully, I learn from the Jesus who gave up himself, his mission, his life in ways that all seemed totally wrong, that the deaths I died may bring new life to the world around me as well.

The Rising

Death the destroyer is not nearly so imponderable a part of life as it may seem. At its worst, it is still an opportunity to start life anew. It is the door through which most of us will walk at least several times in life. What we do with it, drawing on the life and experiences we have had in the life before this one, is both the junction and the challenge of a lifetime. And yet it is out of the dark, wet dust of yesterday that life forever blooms.

When we take hold of life with all its deaths and all its resurrections, life becomes an eternal hotbed of creation given into the hands of the creature so that creation can go on creating.

13. Jesus Is Taken Down from the Cross

The Experience

Now when it is finally, irrevocably over, when there is nothing left to do but to admit the loss, the inevitability of reality takes over. Faith is bruised. Hope is gone. The door to yesterday has clanged shut and we are forever bereft of whole segments of our life. We are alone—the worst word in the English language has descended on our shoulders. And suddenly we begin to realize how limited we ourselves have always been but only now had to admit. We were not meant to be alone.

The insight crushes us to the ground. Where is the rest of me, if not in a coffin of pain in the front of the world, never to be able to hide again?

The realization that death eclipses time, that it alone has the capacity to take past, present and future from us in the same moment is enough to smother the rest of life forever.

Life, we come to understand, is not a monument; it is a crystal ball, fragile and brittle to the touch. The smallest details of life threaten it—a cold turned into pneumonia, a car in the wrong lane, a slip on a ladder, the public words of the charismatic leader, the accumulation of hidden enemies, the exhaustion of the giving heart.

Whatever the enemy, every breath of life becomes a risk subject to the vagaries of time.

Sooner or later we come to understand that life is a gift of momentous proportions but is given without the security of knowing that once achieved it will be impervious to change. A mystery beyond understanding, it comes, at the same time, laden down with the pain of irredeemable and unexplainable loss. Life comes to us as the reckless joy of possibility but it comes, too, with the agonizing awareness that someday, when we least expect it, we may need to let go of it to begin all over again.

The Call

The call to the unknown is the call to trust what is behind the mist of life to come. It is the challenge to believe that in the darkness there is yet another life to be had. Such spiritual gambling is not an easy virtue. Having already been denied the certainty that planning implies, having already lost what appeared to be the very bedrock of our lives, the decision to trust that tomorrow will be better than this worst of days is the least of human instincts.

The willingness to start all over again at any point in life comes with great reservation. "Better to bear the evil that we have than to fly to what we do not know," we say. The inclination to hold on, even to the less than beautiful, is part of being human, part of being inclined to hoard life rather than to live it with arms open and head up, facing the winds of the day and believing that the destination we cannot see is just as good or better than the one to which we have already set the sails of our hearts.

Trust is the gift that makes life exciting. It is the golden thread between the human search for the fullness of life and the heart of God that wills it for us.

The Model

The thirteenth station of the cross with its specter of irrevocable loss, its futile efforts, its wasted dreams, drains the human soul to the point of numbness. Can anything worse be imagined than the death of the ideal? When Jesus is taken down from the cross, when hope dies, when everything we ever wanted gets thrown away, discarded, overlooked, ignored, forgotten, we eat the dust of despair.

We wonder what life was ever about if this is all it comes to, despite all the good will, all our great struggles to have it be otherwise. Then, we realize that only God is God, that we are not in charge of time or truth or the architecture of our definition of the perfect world. Then, we understand: This next step is, like Jesus, to give ourselves over to the arms of God and trust.

The question on which the thirteenth station concentrates us is a straightforward one: Am I prepared to let go of everything I ever wanted so that God's will can come through me in another way?

The Rising

When we reach the point in life where we no longer insist on being able to control all the paltry little situations of life, we are now prepared to be broken open to the life of God, however it comes. At this point, I understand that God will enter my life, my heart, my soul in more ways that I could ever imagine. Rather than through this one spiritual channel, I will begin to find God hidden in new ideas, beckoning me to new beginnings, offering me the grace in the midst of pain to let go. Then and only then, do all the deaths of the past become what they have always been meant to be, simply steps on a road that is never the end, always a new beginning of the never ending, never static search for God.

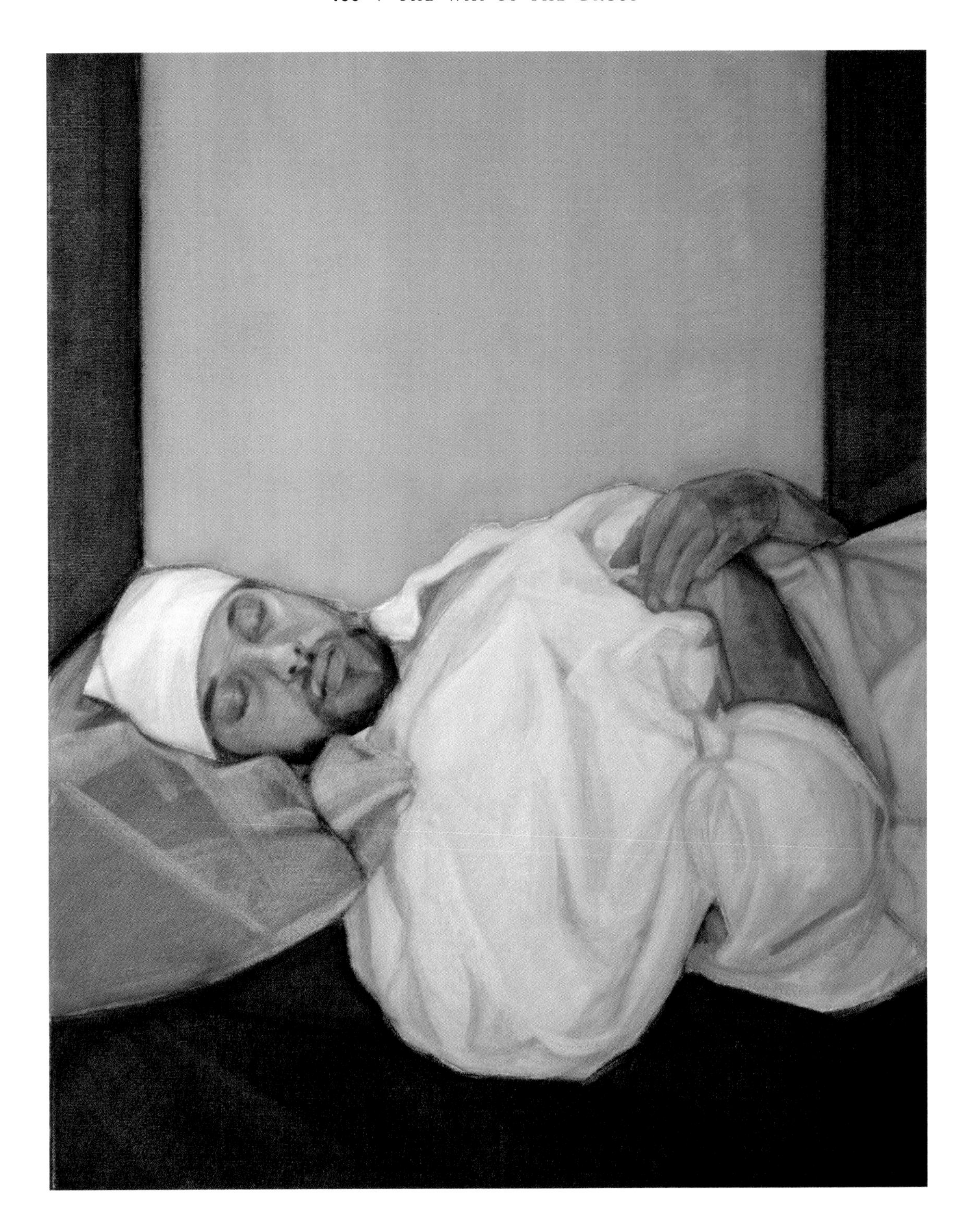

14. Jesus Is Laid in the Tomb

The Experience

Death is not a single action; it is many actions overlapping that haunt, plague, empty the soul of every strand of life and all at the same time. It is a time of mixed emotions. There is a relief that comes when the suffering ends. The one we love cannot be hurt again. And that is good.

But now the focus shifts from them to us. Everything that was glorious and challenging, uplifting and meaningful in life has ended. What is there left for us in life now? Is there the means to go on? And if the means is present, is there yet the will to go on, the energy, the down-deep care of even beginning to go on again?

There is the sense of weightlessness, the thought that life comes down nowhere at all. There is no tomorrow, no yesterday to steer by. All the normal signposts of life—what we do on Mondays, who comes by on Tuesdays, where we'll go for supper on Wednesday, how many will come to the service on Thursday, what project will we start together on Friday—becomes one long gray corridor without color, without light, without hope. The last handful of dirt on the coffin ends whatever is the life of life within us.

It is an awesome moment. There are choices to be made now

that will affect the rest of our lives: We may decide to simply stop where we are, sink into the dust of the soul and wait for the death of the psyche to take the body, too. Or we may make some desultory attempts to keep the old life alive despite the searing reality of it. We may make the life that's left a shrine to the past and ourselves become its keepers.

Then, the stories are all old ones told and retold to whoever will listen, the furniture of the mind's life grows old, always olden, all scenes from years gone by. The plans that were made years ago become the dream that can never be real. Only the brave take the energy of the past and turn it into something else. For them it becomes new again because, they know, it can no longer be the same as it once was. And yet it springs into the future out of the vision of a past that was itself dynamic, never meant to be becalmed by listlessness.

Nevertheless, even if we ourselves are secure—the mortgage is paid, the children are raised, the days are full—there is the eternal gap in life now. The missing populate the present now in ways they never did when they were alive and days were regular and tomorrow was sure.

We find ourselves at the intersection between commitment and desperation. We can begin again or we can give way to despair.

It is precisely then when the tombs of our lives become one thing or another—a shocking propulsion into a world we never foresaw and do not want or a seal on the goodness of life past that demands we give our own life now to the completion of the unfinished journey. Otherwise, what is the value of the past? What was the good of the dream? What is the purpose of life?

It is the tomb itself that presses us to live and to grow out of the best of the past to the rest of the future.

It presses us beyond our stagnant hearts. It is then, at that moment, that the Stations of the Cross take on real meaning.

The Call

We can see now that the call of the Stations of the Cross is not to death and despair at all. The call of the Stations of the Cross to those who walk them, burdened by their own lives, at risk of losing faith, in the very throes of an impenetrable darkness of the heart is to take what is good from the past and go forward with it into a future pulsing with new life.

The Model

The fourteenth station of the cross brings us to grapple with the grace of closure. Some phases of life end and cannot be retrieved. They go by before we're ready to see them go. Worse, their going may feel like ignominy at the time or may even look to the world like failure. Then the finality of loss may sting with grave injustice and may grieve us beyond all telling of it. Yet only in the ability to realize that life goes on from one stage to another, from one kind of presence to another, can we ever come to new life. When Jesus submits to the death of his ministry, when Jesus allows both state and synagogue to still the thunder of his voice, one life ends so that another can begin—ours as well as his—so that the echo of his might thunders on in us.

The Rising

The inauspicious reality of all the resurrections of life is that they all come out of the little deaths of life. When death itself is the ground of resurrection, it is particularly painful, sometimes achingly slow for the transition from death to resurrection to happen.

The truth, however, is that every new tomb signals that, for some-

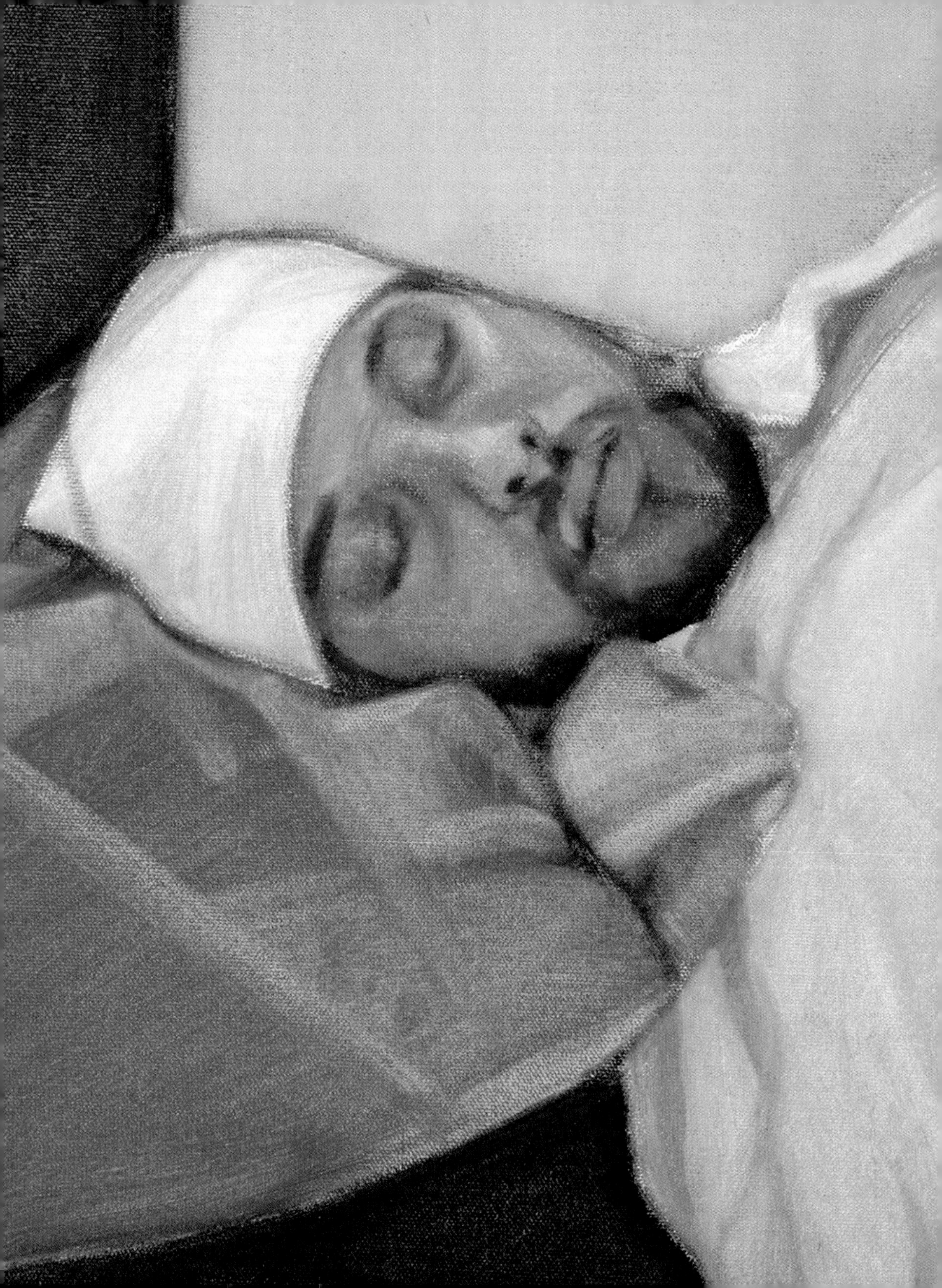

one, another life is about to begin at the edge of it, wanted or not, foreseen or not, planned or not. It is the very nature of tombs to require new life from us.

The resurrection moment at the tomb rises out of the demand that we must leave it alone, fend for ourselves differently now, bring the past to a new kind of life in us. "Death deprives but it also enriches," a wise old monastic said to me when my father died. It took a year or so for me to realize that, indeed, that death brought out of me an entirely new kind of life. It was not an inauspicious moment at all. It was, in fact, a totally auspicious one as is every crucifixion, every tomb. If we will only wait for it.

The question that the fourteenth station of the cross leaves in our soul is a resounding one: Am I able to trust that the tombs of my life are all gateways to resurrection?

15. The Resurrection

The Experience

Perhaps the most difficult—even spiritually dangerous—dimension of the Stations of the Cross is that lacking a sense or slightest awareness of resurrection, they leave the Christian standing at the edge of the tomb. Numb, lost. Bereft. Without a single thought of what comes next. And all of that despite the fact that Christians are not meant to be the people of the cross; Christians are the people of the empty tomb. "We are alleluia people," Augustine writes, "and alleluia is our cry." Perhaps that's true, theologically so. But it is not the final emotional impression of those whose immersion in the life of Jesus centers around the crucifixion in the Stations of the Cross rather than on the overwhelming impact of the resurrection.

The important element in the development of private devotions, regardless how popular, how universal they might be, is that, as a rule, they come out of particular eras and specific instances. They emphasize one dimension of the faith with great particularity. They impress the believer with one facet of the life of Jesus or the church but fail to present the whole picture.

Veneration of the saints brings to our attention the specific strength each of them, as heroes of the faith, demonstrates in the Christian life.

Stanislaus Kostka's courageous act of Christian generosity, for instance. Or Dominic's commitment to catechesis and St. Francis of Assisi's witness to voluntary poverty in a time of growing affluence. The rosary, on the other hand, concentrates on the life of Mary. Adoration of the Blessed Sacrament heightens the place of the Eucharist in the church. Whatever the devotion in question, they all grow out of periods in which each of these devotions was seen to underscore a specific insight or need of the time. In just that way, the Stations of the Cross in times of war and plague, personal sorrow and public reparation, have centered the Christian community on the sufferings of Christ in a suffering world in need of strength to bear the crosses of the time.

The important thing to remember, however, is that we are not meant to see the crucifixion as an end point. We are not to center the entire spiritual life there. There is nothing Christian about treating the crucifixion as the acme of the spiritual pursuit and the focus of our faith. The focus of our faith is the awareness that the Christ who lives beyond the cross calls us beyond it as well. It is the resurrection that brings faith to wholeness, to more than the mere acceptance of the dour reality of life here, to what the church to this day calls "this valley of tears."

We have reason, the resurrection reminds us, to believe in the ultimate blessedness of life even in the midst of its natural sufferings.

Our life, too, the resurrection says, does not end here.

The call of the resurrection is to hope. To know that there is life beyond this life. To know that what we know of blessing here is only a fraction of the life to come.

Beyond our own resurrections into the stream of life to come is a cosmic world that is pulsating with life in its every dimension. What is here, as we know life now—whatever the questions, the challenges, the demands along the way—has been good. We have grown and achieved and enjoyed and loved and been loved in return. What will come in the mystery of time, we see in the quiet face of Jesus, will be even richer, calmer, more fundamentally enlivening than life as we know it now.

In the placid face of Jesus we see the foundational serenity of the

universe, the presence of another life that will make this one, eventually and eternally, fulfilled. We see, too, the marks on his hands that attest to what it takes to come to the whole of life within us: the willingness to grapple with evil, the strength to give ourselves over to love that is not lust, the determination to make our own lives worthwhile for others, and, finally, the courage to refuse to give in to the forces of spiritual slavery around us.

The resurrection, the inner call to the Eternal More, to the sense of undying life within us, is the magnet that keeps us moving through life, in quest of its mystery, in certainty of its truth. Alleluia.